# All That I Need

## Childfree by Choice

*by*

# Natasja Rose

ISBN: 9781086377873

The views expressed in this book are the opinions of the author and the contributors, and not intended as a reflection on anyone but that individual. Names are used with permission, or replaced by a pseudonym for annonyminity.

# TABLE OF CONTENTS

# INTRODUCTION

Having kids is not for everyone.

Whether you like children, hate them, or just have other priorities in life, everyone seems to have an opinion on your lack of spawn and a iron-clad conviction that you will change your mind eventually.

After the umpteenth time of being assured by relatives that I will change my mind, random strangers looking sympathetic while assuming that I can't, and blank confusion followed by "but you're so good with kids!", I decided that the Childfree State was clearly another thing that needed to be experience-splained to the general public.

Research was gathered by way of a short-answer survey, sent out to people who responded to a general request on social media. For the sake of accuracy, I have excluded those responses who stated that they want kids but couldn't have them, or were planning to adopt.

Both of those are valid stances, but outside of the scope of actively choosing not to have children.

Because of certain other responses, mostly unsolicited, I feel the need to emphasise that neither this book nor the research survey are meant as an attack upon those who chose to have children. All opinions expressed are those of the individual.

Thanks go to Wendy, Amy, Frieda*, Anne*, Jane*, Wendy (different one), Christine, Sky, Wendy (Again), Myranda, Betty, Lyndal, Chuck, Tam, Rose, Cassandra, Michelle, Louise and Darren.

*The interviewee wished to remain anonymous or under an assumed name. This can be for professional or personal reasons, and should not be viewed negatively.

# EXPERIENCES

Everyone has different experiences, both in why they chose not to have children of their own and in how people and families reacted to that choice.

Some families and friends are supportive, some are disbelieving and convinced that you'll change your mind, some outright state that you're being selfish or will regret it.

**What is your experience of choosing not to have children? Why did you make that choice and how do people react?**

I actually really like children, and adore my niece and pseudo-niblings (shortened, gender-neutral term for nieces and nephews). I like the ability to give them back at the end of the day even more.

In my teens, I thought I would one day have kids, because it was expected and I saw how happy my aunts and uncles were as grandparents. As I grew older, I took a long, hard look at what would be involved, and had a very frank talk with my doctor. He said that to have any chance of carrying a pregnancy to term, I'd need to go off my epilepsy medication. No, thank you.

There's also the small issue of me being Asexual, working a job that does not match up with single parenthood, and not having the money for IVF, let alone the financial stability to raise a child.

My parents actually took my decision quite well, and made sure that I knew they would support me in whatever I decided. My Aunts still stare blankly and ask when I'm going to settle down and start reproducing every time they see me. My (male) manager asked me how I could possibly feel fulfilled without children, and wasn't I worried about having no-one to take care of me when I was old?

-*Natasja*


I have always known I had no interest on being a parent. My experience of childhood is that my parents were devoted to my sister and me, and (perhaps selfishly) I decided I couldn't handle that degree of overwhelming responsibility, for if I were to have children and follow my parents' example, it would mean living and breathing purely for my children. It was a really big deal and not to be taken lightly! So I thought about it as soon as I was old enough to have such thoughts, and concluded that would not be my path.

People historically have reacted by assuring me that I will change my mind eventually. These claims have petered off as I aged, and then redoubled a few years ago when I married. I have always said to people that on the contrary, if I were to accidentally fall pregnant I would have it aborted. I think it's sensible to think about this scenario before it happens, as I imagine the pregnant female body would be awash with hormones of a pro-motherhood nature, and that would really not be a state in which to make an unbiased decision.

Also amusing is that my partner and I had been together for years prior to our marriage. Friends and family suddenly asking if we would now have a baby seemed utterly bizarre, given I was nearing 40 by then, coupled with the fact that we are not religious at all. Surely if we had planned a child we wouldn't have waited that long? Who cares about 'within wedlock' these days?

*-Wendy*

Most people say "I will change my mind." Which gets on my nerves as people who are close to me Family and collar friends know I won't. The worst response I ever got was from a doctor, I asked if I could have the 10-year coil put in but she insisted that I have the five year as it makes it easier to have children. When I told her I didn't want children, she said "What is wrong with you? What has happened in your past to make you feel this way?" at this point I got very angry and defended myself to which she responded with "you are getting very defensive." With a smug look on her face.

*-Amy*

I've never wanted kids, from start to end, I don't like small children at all, I find them annoying and frustrating and boring and tedious, and personally I find the idea of gestating a parasite inside me ABSOLUTELY HORRIFYING, it's a literal nightmare situation for me - pregnancy, birth process, raising a baby, raising a toddler, raising a child, dealing with teenagers, NONE of it has ever appealed to me. Most people react pretty fine, I'm fortunate that my Dad doesn't care if me and my siblings have kids (he is much too busy gallivanting around with his younger girlfriend, and travels a lot himself) and my 2 other siblings and I are all in our 30s and none of us look to ever have kids, so I have people around me who totally understand. I've been pretty lucky in that respect. I have close friends (most of them are childless geeks like me) and I'm very close to whole my family, Im surrounded by amazing people and very fortunate they never bother me about kids.

My boyfriend is my dream man, I'm so happy and in love with him - he does already have kids (11 & 13, so they are already developed people and aren't bratty at all) so he absolutely definitely doesn't want more, which is PERFECT. He has his kids part time and I only tend to see them maybe 1 day a month on average, I catch up with him every other week, so we keep our relationships mostly separate which works beautifully for me as I need lots of ME-TIME space anyway, which I get when he is busy doing the dad stuff. They are nice kids and thankfully at that age they are reasonable autonomous, he doesn't require my help with them and said from the start he isn't looking for a step-mum for them, just someone who can be a friend. It's a great set-up as far as I'm concerned.

-Frieda*

When I was younger I just assumed I would have kids, like my parents had me & my brother. I wanted 2 bio kids, plus maybe 1 that was adopted. The older I got & the more that I realized & understood the immense burden & hassle that having kids is, that number of kids slowly shrunk. 1 bio kid & 1 adopted. Then just 1 bio. Then only 1 adopted. Then none at all. By the time my teens were done, I had decided to be childfree.

Whenever I tell people that I'm not having kids, the majority of them look skeptical. I still have people telling me that I'll change my mind, even after knowing me for years & years & seeing that I still have no kids. I find that when I tell them my age, it becomes more believable to them, since I don't look my age, but it's annoying that I even have to do that at all.

-Anne*

- It's a big responsibility to have a kid. You have to protect them from a world full of evil and I don't think humans are qualified to do that. We don't even know how to take care of ourselves late on another immature human.

- Why? Because I didn't want the responsibility of raising a child when I knew I was not going to be able to raise a perfect human in a perfect safe world.

- I have been told I am selfish. I will change my mind. That's a lonely life. Don't you want to have something that is yours and has your genes.

-*Jane**


I have never wanted children. Never wanted to play with dolls as a child would rather animals.
-*Wendy*


I made the choice so I have freedom - both financially and schedule wise
-*Christine*

What is your experience of choosing not to have children? Why did you make that choice and how do people react?

My own mental health on top of the fact that my family is just shit. I don't want to be the reason another human being suffers in this world so I refuse to make more. And I refuse to give my family the satisfaction of knowing their bloodline was continued through me. It's the biggest f you to all of them :) my family doesn't like that I don't want kids. And some friends question why and assume that anyone that doesn't have kids when they turn 20 are immediately into the party scene for whatever reason

-Sky


I've had the freedom to live my life and follow my own path.

-Wendy


I have many reasons. The most being I have just never liked/wanted children. I like the freedom I have knowing I only answer to myself and that I'm not being financially drained by dependents.

I've noticed I've lived a far more stress free and happier life getting to work on my own development as a person as opposed to my friends and family whip have multiple children at young ages who seem miserable in their lives in comparison to me.

I made the choice because at the end of the day it's just not for me, I don't need to reproduce and put my body through that to be fulfilled in life. For the most part people I'm close to now have responded favorably or atleast with some understanding from most of my peers and family, though it has taken some time for people to start understanding I'm not going to have kids. My mother in law has been very supportive of my husband and I being childfree. My own mother seems to have baby fever since my neice was born and I'm sure I'll be pestered by her at some point to give her another grandbaby unless my sister continues to have more kids which she likely will to satiate my mother. I do have a lot of people tell me "I might change my mind" but the longer I've been adamant with people about my choices and why, most of them have been understanding.

*-Myranda*

I knew in my heart I didn't want children since I was very little, I think I properly realized it when I was 10 years old. At first everyone said I'd change my mind... that obviously didn't happen.

My main reason is I love my freedom

*-Betty*


Marriage and babies was the plan for a long time, though I believe it was more because I thought it was expected rather than an actual desire to have children. I always thought the entire process of procreation seemed kinda gross and quite uncomfortable/painful, but it took a while before I actually connected that with having children and realised that I wasn't actually interested. It took me a long time to realise that not getting married or having children was actually an option.

My family reacted fairly well to my decision, though that was after some fairly lengthy explanation and a lot of questions. When people ask when I'm getting married and/or having kids, I just tend to just stun people into silence with a super chirpy "Never!"

I am super grateful to my sister for my nephew though - he is the best follow-up question deterrent/distraction. He's also super adorable, so that's awesome too.

*-Lyndal*

When I was 5 years old and found out that there were orphans with no parents I asked my mother if we could adopt some. She said "No" because she only wants her own children. That is when I realized my mother was very selfish and did not care about others.

Also when I found out that animals are killed for humans to eat, I tried to be a vegetarian several times without success. I would get very lethargic after a couple of weeks without any meat products.

Dr. Mercola and several other doctors have proven that very low percentage of people can be healthy as vegetarians. Therefore most people must eat meat to be healthy. And if both the biological mother and biological father were healthy vegetarians their whole lives, that does not mean that the children that they spawn would be healthy as a vegetarian. Knowing that, for every new human that is spawned Millions of chickens and cows will have to be murdered to feed that new child throughout his lifetime. And millions more animals will have to be murdered to feed that humans spawn. So creating new people that never asked to be born is not only immoral, it is The Epitome of Selfishness. Therefore it is impossible for good people to create families by breeding. If they were truly good people Who wanted children they would adopt orphans who are already on this planet that are being tortured and neglected every day because they are orphans. A good person who wanted children would adopt the orphans to give them a chance of having a decent life instead of selfishly breeding More humans that never asked to be born in the first place knowing that thier selfish breeding will cause millions of more animals to have to be murdered to feed their spawn. breeders are the ones that are destroying the planet. It is the non-breeders that are saving the planet and doing good. The Nikola Teslas' and mother Theresas' never breed, but all the selfish cockroaches and shysters breed.

https://dailycaller.com/2013/02/26/in-memoir-ashley-judd-said-it-was-selfish-for-people-to-procreate/

I used birth control and my husband got a vasectomy.

My sisters and my mother kept telling me "You should have your own kids/get pregnant because you have blue green eyes and are intelligent." My sisters were very selfish and self-centered like my mother. They also said that since since brown eyed people are reproducing at a much faster rate than blue/green eyed people that blue/green eyed people should be trying to produce more babies. LOL!!! Their selfishness makes them think this is a race of the different ethnic races!!

They got angry when I mentioned that more animals have to be murdered to feed more children being born.

-*Chuck*

Wonderful. I do not like children & never wanted that burden. Many people acted like I was inconveniencing them by not having children or that it made them mad. Some were jealous.

-*Tam*

It's been an eye-opening lifestyle to choose, experiencing the different reactions of people and society as a whole.

A number of reasons, really, but all boiling down to I don't want to. I've been fairly blessed so far in my experience with people and their reactions, most people are respectful.

-*Rose*

I was always very good with kids, so growing up I always assumed I would have kids if my own. That then morphed into no bio kids, but maybe I'll adopt. At the age of 15 though, right when I figured out I was clinically depressed and could barely take care of myself, I realized that I could never take care of a kid to the level they should be taken care of.

My parents supported my decision, but they were saddened by it. They were the only opinion I really cared about. Whenever the topic of kids comes up now, I just say I can't have kids (which I can't, had my tubes removed) and that usually stops the discussion any further.

-*Cassandra*

I live in an urban area with lots of under 40s. Everyone is very chill about it and sees what a great life we lead. WE don't need to explain much.

-*Michelle*

I initially used this to break up with a boyfriend who in hindsight was emotionally manipulative. He always wanted kids and had said that not wanting kids would be a deal breaker. I quickly realised after we broke up that child-free was the right choice for me anyway. I could do a solid 10-minute PowerPoint presentation explaining and listing reasons why I don't want children

-*Louise*

I come from a huge catholic family so it was just expected I'd breed like the rest of them. I think I was totally turned off the idea at about 13 when my cousins used to sit around the dining room table discussing birth stories - just revolting.

*-Debbie*

Ever since my early teens, I have never had any desire to have children. As a result, I have been called selfish; been told that I'd change my mind (I never have); and been advised that having children was inevitable (it wasn't).

*-Darren*

# THE GOOD

There are a lot of good things that come with being child-free. Less financial stress (raising a kid is expensive!), more travel options, flexibility in your daily life... the list is very extensive.

Everyone has different reasons for choosing not to have children, but the general consensus is that the good points far outweigh the bad.

**What is the best thing about being Childless?**

You know what's really awesome? The ability to jump on a plane to another state or country, or go for a three-hour drive to visit friends, and the only things I need to worry about are if I've packed enough medication and remembered to turn on the alarm.

When my grandfather died recently, at the beginning of the school term, I could call the airline, switch my travel dates for two weeks early, and be on a plane in time for the funeral. (Also, I really don't want to imagine what 30+ hours of travel, with layovers measured in less than two hours and red-eye departures, would be like with a small child. I was wrecked travelling solo!)

Also, I can take on the weekend and night shifts at work, and rack up the penalty rates. I don't have to stress about dropping kids off or picking them up before a shift, or get up early to make sure they're up in time.

*(I do get accused of being "heartless" when telling my co-workers to get off their mobile phones while on shift. If their kids have an actual emergency, they can call their fathers. I would like to stop having to deal with a dozen complaints in a week, just because your pre-teen children can't manage getting ready for school without calling you for every tiny thing. I still have no idea how that one twit managed to claim that running to answer the phone in the middle of a manual transfer was justifiable with a straight face.)*

*-Natasja*


Freedom. Choices with only 2 of us to consider. The ability to take risks. The ability to travel without it being a massive rigmarole. In fact, the ability to simply visit the supermarket without it being a nightmare.

-*Wendy*

Freedom! I seriously get bored so easy and I know for a fact that I would regret/resent a child for taking up my time, I am okay bring on my own and I am good seeing friends! But I love the choice, I want to live for me! Not someone else.

-*Amy*

Im way too selfish - I LOVE to sleep for 10+ hours a day, I love to travel where and when I want to, I can do weekend trips at the drop of a hat, I can go out and play Dungeons & Dragons til 3 in the morning any time I want, I don't have to factor anyone else into my decision making, I get to keep my body in shape, I get to spend my money on exactly what I want and nothing else, I'm completely free - there is LITERALLY NO DOWNSIDE as far as I can see about remaining child-free.

-*Frieda**

I'm an introvert, & I love being alone. The thought of having some kid completely reliant on me, whining, complaining, eating my food, having to clean up after them, having to always watch them, having to spend money on them, always having to encourage them, pretending that that they're so special, being pregnant in the first place…nothing about being a parent appeals to me at all. I love my peace, quiet, & freedom. Being childfree is a no-brainer for me.

*-Anne**

Being responsible of only myself, the freedom to go anywhere I want without worrying about another human beings welfare do what I want when I want and be flexible

*-Jane**

I do what I want

*-Wendy*

It's awesome and you have a lot of freedom plus your bank account will thank you lol. I'm a financial coach and when I've done my retirement modeling, I wouldn't be able to reach retirement early if I had kids

*-Christine*

I can have pets and make sure I'm ok. I can spend more time with my boyfriend and we only have to feed ourselves

*-Sky*

Knowing I've not contributed to overpopulation

*-Wendy*

The freedom and the money saved. I can go on vacation or go out whenever I want without having to worry about a babysitter or being responsible for a good the entire time.

*-Myranda*

Childfree, not childless. freedom is the best thing... in every sense of the word I'm free, which can also be a bit scary sometimes as I have to forge a life of my own.

*-Betty*

Not being solely responsible for another life. Often, I can barely take care of myself, much less anyone else.

*-Lyndal*


I don't have any guilt because I did Not create another person which would have created a bigger demand to kill more animals in the future. And also did not create a bigger demand to use other resources.

*-Chuck*


I can spend my time & money as I choose.

*-Tam*


The freedom to feel like I have my own life, and am not going to screw another human up for the rest of the future world to have to deal with.

*-Rose*


You mean child free right? I can stay out as late as I want, the only thing I have to come home to is a cat wondering why her routine has been interrupted! But she gets over that pretty quickly once she gets her rub down.

-*Cassandra*

Freedom to do what I want to do, free time, no dependents to worry about financially.

-*Michelle*

Silence and money are the ones you see most often in child-free forums I think. I'd add to that peace, quiet, control over my life, the ability to focus on myself (still learning how to take care of myself tbh)

-*Louise*

No screaming bratty kids, I'm not maternal in the slightest, I detest kids

-*Debbie*

Having my life to myself, and much less fear and stress.

-*Darren*

# THE BAD

Some people have no regrets about being child-free, but choice means taking the good with the (occasional) bad.

Not bad enough to make you change your mind, but perhaps nostalgia or regret for a missed experience, or perceived disappointment from those close to you.

**What is something you regret about being child-free?**

I don't really regret anything, but there are occasional downsides. I see how happy my parents are with being grandparents to my niece, and wish that they could have enjoyed it sooner. I regret the lessened contact with friends who gravitate to playdates and parent social groups, and have less time and opportunity to go out, because they're limited by finding a babysitter.

I sometimes wonder what parenthood would have been like, how my adoration of the niblings might have translated with a child of my own, but not enough to actually go through with it myself.

*-Natasja*

I am aware that there are experiences that I will never have, because I have seen my sister bear two children and know that the "second-hand" journey of aunthood is different to motherhood. However I still believe I made the right choice for me.

*-Wendy*

My regrets in life have nothing to do with children, for example I wish I took singing lessons early on in life. I wish I took dance lessons as a child… when it comes to children. I just cannot be bothered, the closest thing I can think to regret is maybe not spending as much time with my nephews and niece. But I'm satisfied that they know who I am and I'm the fun Auntie, but I don't enjoy spending long periods with them.

*-Amy*

I don't have a single regret in that regard! Ive had one pregnancy termination years ago, and I don't regret it one bit. If I was unsure about my stance I might have regrets, but the older I get, the firmer in this way of thinking I am, I have no room whatsoever in my life to raise a child, and I know if I was forced into that situation, I would regret and resent the child for ruining my perfect selfish happy life.

-Frieda*


Nothing whatsoever. I'm a smug childfree person. I think about my childfree future & I wriggle with joy. LOL!

-Anne*


Not having a mini me who looks like me. Loving another human being unconditional because I made them, Just showing love to an innocent child that deserves it. I am angry our world stole that from me because of how evil it is.

-Jane*


I regret nothing although I am scared I will die alone and my cat might eat me

-Wendy

None

-*Christine*

Nothing. The people I actually consider friends don't shove their kids down everyone's throats 24/7. The one mombie I know I actively avoid anyway. I already know my stance on kids and so do most of my friends

-*Sky*

Not being louder & prouder about it earlier. Missing years of advocasy

-*Wendy*

I don't regret anything per say but it had kind of sucked that I have lost several friendships because once they had kids and became mombies we no longer had anything in common. It also sucks that I seem to get secluded from my family because I don't have kids, my sister's babysit for each other and do stuff together with their kids, I'm never really asked to go or do anything anymore because I've made it known is rather be around adults than hanging around kids all the time and I'm not wanting to babysit for them because it's not exactly a fair trade when I don't have kids for them to take if needed and I don't even know how to entertain a child for any length of time.

Basically it bothers me a little that I get left out but overall if I'm getting left out from hanging around kids and mombies I'm fine with that.

-*Myranda*

No regrets. If anything I'd have mild curiosity and mild missing out sensation for certain events that would be fun with kids, for instance Christmas and Santa Claus, elf on the shelf etc. I'd love to be able to be mommy for one holiday and then give the kids back and continue with my fabulous life

-*Betty*

Now that I have a nephew to spoil, any regrets I used to feel have mostly vanished. I still wonder what it might be like to have a little person that was just like me from time to time, but I'm okay with not knowing.

-*Lyndal*

I don't have any regrets about not being a selfish breeder. But I wish humans would support non-breeders instead of stealing their hard-earned money to give to the selfish breeders.

FINALLY a politician that speaks the REAL Truth! Senator Leyonhjelm said making childless people pay for other people's choices was not just unfair, but in some cases cruel.

"Some people are childless by choice and are happy with that choice. There is no moral case to make them subsidise other people's choices.

For some people, childlessness is not a choice; it is a great sadness. Forcing them to hand over money to more fortunate people is like charity in reverse. It's like making people in wheelchairs pay for other people's running shoes. Most welfare payments for parents should be abolished. The government is not your parent or your spouse — get over it," he told the Senate on Monday.

"To the childless people of Australia I want to say, on behalf of this parliament, thank you for being childless. You work for more years and become more productive than the rest of Australia. You pay thousands and thousands of dollars more tax than other Australians. You get next to no welfare and your use of public health services is minimal.

But you pay when other people get pregnant, you pay when they give birth, you pay when they stay at home to look after their offspring, you pay for the child's food, clothing and shelter, you pay when the child goes to child care and you pay when the child goes to primary and secondary school. And then you pay when it goes to university."

*-Chuck*

I have no regrets about being Childfree.

*-Tam*

That I won't experience the positive aspects of having kids, and would miss out of the experience of having a baby.

*-Rose*

About not having kids? Maybe not being able to pass down what I've learned easily? But that's what volunteering is for, right? There are ways to impart what I've learned to the next generation without the burden of having your own child.

-*Cassandra*

The idea of having grown kids seems nice but can't really skip that first 20 years.

-*Michelle*

I may or may not regret not knowing how to deal with kids when I go visit my brother and his baby girl in December. Dunno yet. I rarely bump into children.

-*Louise*

I regret a lot of things, not breeding is not one of them.

-*Debbie*

Nothing - deciding that I am child-free has been one of the best decisions I have ever made.

-*Darren*

# I WISH YOU KNEW...

A big part of the misunderstanding and stigma surrounding the choice to be childfree is the inability to comprehend why someone might make that choice.

In the face of that mental disconnect, the automatic wish is that the other person could put themselves in your shoes, and know what you thought and felt.

So, here is what we wish parents knew about why we chose to be child-free.

**What is something you wish other people knew about being childfree by choice?**

That I didn't choose not to have children because I'm sick, or broken, or mentally unwell, or selfish. That it's a choice I made for myself, because I believe that it's better not to have kids in the first place, than to have them and abandon or resent them.

I'm happy being the fun aunt that kids squeal and run to greet, but nothing in the world will ever make me agree to be a parent.

(I've split up with two partners over this already. Yes, I'm serious.)

-*Natasja*

It gives me more opportunity to be a good aunt to my sister's kids. If I had my own family I would have a lot less energy to spend on them.

-*Wendy*

That it's a valid choice! I don't like how having children is normalised and it's so alien for people not to want them. I don't understand why people can't just accept it.

-*Amy*

That it fucking ROCKS! I wish people knew that you don't HAVE to do what society says you should. Ive met people who when I told them about my situation, have straight up told me if they could go back and do it all over again, they would choose NOT to have their children. That is mind-blowing, and I feel so sorry for them, imagine waking up each day RESENTING your own child. Imagine being the child and KNOWING that if your parents could go back in time, they would wipe you out of existence! That's no small thing, I wish ore people knew that its perfectly OK to not have a child. That a family can be 2 people and no more. I love my man so much, Id hate to bring a 3$_{rd}$ party into it that would take up all of our attention and time and then never have any time for each other. I cant think of anything sadder.

-Frieda*


That it's a real option for life. That it's a decision that we don't take lightly, & often reached after extensive thought & consideration (which is more than can be said for most breeders & their "Oops" babies). That it doesn't mean that we hate kids or would do harm to them, it just means that we choose not to ever give birth to them or be personally responsible for them. That many of us (maybe even most) go out of our way to make sure that we never get pregnant in the first place. We don't all just have a bunch of abortions in our wake, & that's why we've managed to not have children. No, idiot. I'm just serious about my choice & I conduct myself accordingly.

-*Anne**

We are not selfish we just respect life and are responsible adults for being realistic and not being selfish like breeders.

-*Jane**

I'm a server I hate when people ask if I have children it's rude!

-*Wendy*

Before having kids, make sure it's really what YOU want and not because you're pressured by parents or family.

-*Christine*

That I don't hate kids. I just don't want any of my own. Also, no one is entitled to pay attention to your kid. They're your responsibility. Stop trying to make people feel guilty for not waving back to your crotch demon

-*Sky*

That it is a choice. That they do not have to follow the cultural script

-*Wendy*

That there's nothing wrong with not wanting children. It's actually a very responsible decision for most people. Most of us are jyst wanting/able to undergo such a lifelong intense commitment (financially, emotionally, or with your time). It's far more responsible than someone having multiple children they can't afford and needing government assistance to care for the children. Childfree people save the taxpayers money and we boost the economy with spending our extra money that doesn't go towards childcare.

-*Myranda*

How amazing CF life is and all the research around the effect of children on marriage and life satisfaction.

*-Betty*

You don't need a partner or children to be complete or accomplished. You are not broken or crazy or weird if you don't want kids. It doesn't mean you have any more or less love to share.

Being an aunt is no less worthy than being a mother, nor does it mean you love the child less. Family is made up of the people you love and who love you in return, it doesn't have to be blood-related.

*-Lyndal*

I wish that everyone would admit the truth..that it is the Non-breeders that are the heroes saving the planet, and so non-breeders should be supported instead of ripped off and taken advantage of.

*-Chuck*

I wish that being CF was given as an option to young people. They shouldn't be made to believe that children are a requirement in their future.

*-Tam*

Few people ever experience the stigma associated with choosing a lifestyle so out of the accepted norm. People who choose to be childfree are seen as outcasts and treated as if they're diseased, not too dissimilar to other alternative lifestyle choices, and it's difficult to simply exist as a normal human in society.

*-Rose*

That more young people were told that it's a perfectly understandable way to live. There should be no stigma around the idea of not having a child. Go through the pro/con list if you have to - but make sure it's YOUR decision, not society's.

*-Cassandra*

I love kids, just not willing to dedicate my entire life to specific kids, too much time and effort that I'd prefer to spend on myself, my partner, adventure and caring for others who already exist in the world.

*-Michelle*

That not everyone is cut out to be a parent. There are far too many parents who should never have had children for various reasons. And for those calling child-free-by-choice people selfish ... the vast majority of decisions that humans make are selfish. So chill on that front.

*-Louise*


We aren't selfish, we put a lot of thought into not breeding, we don't have a huge disposable income, we have bills and mortgages etc exactly like breeders to pay for.

*-Debbie*


Not everyone wants, or needs, to have children.

*-Darren*

# FINAL THOUGHTS

Because the survey questions addressed specific aspects of the child-free state, this is the place for closing statements, and any opinions not covered by the previous questions.

**Any final thoughts?**

This actually gave me a lot of new insight, and I think it was a very productive discussion to have. I'm happy with the life that I've chosen, and wouldn't have it any other way.

On a side note, if you're on the fence about kids, I do recommend having that discussion with your partner sooner rather than later. Not on the first date, but definitely before your one-year anniversary.

*-Natasja*

I don't think so, but I welcome any further questions on the subject.

-Wendy

I love being child-free, its absolutely the life for me and I will shout it from the roof-tops any chance I get! Life is all about choices, and I know Ive absolutely made all the right ones for me.

-Frieda*

I'm 42 & childfree for life. I made this decision a long time ago. I don't regret my decision & I never will.

-Anne*

I truly want people to consider stopping procreations. And I want it to be a law enforced by the government. Where people are going sterilized at birth. I was very happy about the law in China but of course humans will always be humans and the law caused so much pain for women. Being forced to abort babies (because it's not a gender husband wanted) to try again for mostly a boy.

-Jane*

Live your best life. Kids are not for everyone!

-*Wendy*

Nothing wrong with having kids if that's what they really want. I hate working hard to fund another human being that most likely won't pay back what I spent on them

-*Christine*

I enjoyed this survey. It was short and to the point :)

-*Sky*

I've observed over the years that once others realise I'm actively not having kids, they fall into two groups. The ones who suddenly want to portray parenthood as nirvana... Or they confide how bad a choice it was because they know I'll not judge them for it

-*Wendy*

I'm from Alabama. Which just passed the most stringent abortion ban in the country. While I don't personally believe abortion should just be used as a regular form of birth control I do feel like laws like this have been passed to target childfree people like myself in an attempt to force us into being parents even if we're responsible because birth control can fail. It may seem like I'm being paranoid to some people but I feel like this group can understand my position on how laws like these seem to be more in favor of forced birth against the will of the mother.

*-Myranda*

None

*-Betty*

Family is made up of the people you love and who love you in return, it doesn't have to be blood-related.

*-Lyndal*

The bible verses state God is Pro-abortion. God even shares

his magic recipe for abortions:  Numbers 5:15-22. According to the bible God does NOT consider a human to be alive or of any value until 1 month

AFTER birth. Since God is pro-abortion, you can't blame others for being pro-abortion.

Most unwanted children that are born end up in prostitution camps repeatedly raped everyday and die very young even though the adoption agencies claimed the children were going to good families. The responsible thing to use both control.

Anyone who tells you to not get an abortion should be held responsible to pay for all the child's expenses for 18 years to prevent it from being a financial burdan.

Over 95% of humans are Narcissistic Psychopaths. Even though there are MILLIONS of orphans waiting to be adopted, over 95% of humans insist on breeding more children into this world instead of adopting orphans. Their mentality: "It's all about ME, MY Genes and MY mini-ME's". For each child that is born it will require that about 10,000 chickens are murdered to feed it. Human breeders think their genes are the only thing that matters on this planet and THOUSANDS of more animals should be murdered to feed their offspring. Humans have so grossly overpopulated the planet that they have taken over most the arable lands crowding out the rest of the animals, which then forces the farm animals to live in cramped tiny spaces and force fed to grow them to feed the reproducing masses. Breeding is the EPITOME of SELFISHNESS. Human Breeders are Narcissistic Psychopaths.

-*Chuck*

Having large families should be treated like smoking, alcoholism, drugs; it should be frowned upon. It's bad for our environment & society. We need to pressure our peers to limit births, if we want to save our planet.

There needs to be a full blown campaign about being CF. Show the reasons that people have for being CF: financial, mental, emotional, medical, etc. If people choose to have a family later, if their situation improves, there are so many kids in the system, who are available for adoption. There's no need to continue to add to the overpopulation problem.

-*Tam*

I hope this helps - the childfree community deserves to become more normalized.

-*Rose*

The carbon footprint that you leave by bring a child into the world needs to be brought up more. In the world we are in today, with humanity reaching the boiling point with Mother Earths tolerance, people need to be aware of just the environmental affects of a child.

-*Cassandra*

Wish people didn't feel so threatened by childfree people as if our decision was an attack on them. Their defensiveness is exhausting.

-*Michelle*

Everyone is unique and there is not a single template that you can apply to most people. It just doesn't work. I wish people would hear each other out more often before making harsh and unfair judgments.

-*Louise*

More people should actually THINK about breeding, the world would be far better off for it, the world is so over populated.

-*Debbie*

As time has passed, I think it's great that being child-free is becoming more and more acceptable.

-*Darren*

# Author Profile

The 'Living Diversity' Series started in a small cafe, with a small group of people trying to out-ignorant each other over certain issues. In lieu of throwing her milkshake at them for being Excessively Stupid in a Public Forum and getting kicked out of her favourite writing venue, Natasja started working on anecdotal books to break the stigma.

Natasja has been writing since a very young age, though those notebooks have been lost in the Old Schoolbooks Cupboard and (hopefully) will never see the light of day.
Most of her stories, published or otherwise, began life as conversations with friends that sparked an idea that grew into a story or poem.

Her publishing adventures started with poems and short stories in focus newsletters like ABA and AMBA, and online sites like Readwave, before finally taking a chance with self-publishing.

Natasja Rose lives and works in Sydney, Australia, but travels whenever she can afford it and has the time.

Her greatest wish is to visit all the places in the world that inspired her writing as a child, and create new stories for new inspirations.

# FROM THE SAME AUTHOR

## Captive Hearts

No one was entirely sure what had started the conflict with the Grey Mountains, only that there was no end in sight.

When Danae, one of the Vale's most powerful Healers, is taken prisoner in a raid, she finds an unexpected protector: Torrin, the Mountain King's nephew. In fear for her life, Danae is determined to hate the man responsible for her capture, but his kindness and compassion make it increasingly difficult.

Torrin hadn't expected to find himself in charge of a prisoner, especially such a difficult one. He hadn't expected to find her defiance so attractive either. If only she wasn't his prisoner...

In a tale of intrigue, rivalry and love, duty and reason war with uncertain hearts to form a gripping romance.

**Now Available in Kindle Ebook and Paperback**

# *THE HIGHWAYMAN'S LEGACY*

Being a Psychic sucks.

It would probably be worse if Tina Barnes had to listen to every random thought that crossed people's mind, but witnessing the death of every person who died in a spectacularly gory fashion is no picnic, either. Being on a tour of Historically Significant (read: haunted) locations isn't really helping.

Oh, and did she mention the supernatural soap opera of two ghosts possessing random people in their bid for a Happily Ever After that usually ends with the hosts dying?

Because that's happening, too.

In a chilling tale of ghostly romance, friendship and fed-up psychics, what was meant to be a normal holiday tour takes a potentially deadly turn into a race against time.

**Book One of Ghostly Travels**

**Available in Kindle ebook and Paperback**

# *Eternity's Invitation*

Dealing with her best friend being possessed by the ghost of a star-crossed lover was just the beginning.

Returning to a place where she swore she would never set foot again, Tina Barnes is once again dragged kicking and screaming into the realm of the Supernatural.

At least she has company this time.

In the gripping sequel to 'The Highwayman's Legacy', re-join the usual suspects in a series of ghostly murders that have nothing to do with star-crossed lovers....

And everything to do with destroying anyone who has the potential to stop them.

**Book Two of Ghostly Travels**

**Available in Kindle ebook and Paperback**

# All You Can Be

*Living With Aspergers, by Aspies and those who love them*

Asperger's Syndrome affects different people in different ways, from Aspies themselves, to people who have friends or family with the condition.

This is a collection of stories and anecdotes, ranging from the good things about being Aspie, to common coping strategies, to media misrepresentation and how it affects people of all ages and backgrounds.

Being Aspie is far from being all fun and games, but there are definitely far worse things to be.

**Available in Kindle ebook and Paperback**

# All That We Are

*The Asexuality Spectrum, or Love Without Sex*

We live in a very sexualised society, where sex without love is common, but love without sex seems to shock people.

In this book, we will discuss the spectrum of Asexuality, as viewed by the people who live it. This is a collection of anecdotes, ranging from discovering your sexuality, to common misconceptions and prejudice, and basic definitions of the different terms

Being diverse might come with its problems, but what's the point if you can't be yourself?

**Available in Kindle ebook and Paperback**

# The Lost Collection

A place for my poems, short stories and other things that didn't quite merit a book of their own.

You will find short plays for all ages, parody songs, fictional monologues for historical figures, and much more.

Read about Boudicca of the Iceni and the Nika Riots, the woes of an average schoolgirl, the best way to derail a science vs theology debate, and what happens when nursery rhymes go bad.

Whether laughing at comedy or crying over tragedy, this anthology will keep you entertained through to the end.

**Available in Kindle ebook and Paperback**

# The Temporarily-Misplaced

## Collection

More Short Stories, interspaced here and there with the occasional monologue and poem, that didn't quite make it into novels of their own.

Some of them might at a later date, but for now, you can read them here.

Read about the Adventures of Codename Granny, the origins of mermaids, space exploration that doesn't quite go as planned, and reincarnated soulmates that don't always end in Happily Ever After.

A sequel, of sorts, to 'The Lost Collection'.

**Available in Kindle Ebook and Paperback**

# The Writing Prompt Collection

Short stories, plus the occasional monologue and poem, inspired by writing prompts.

Read about the night-time protectors, a different take on the gingerbread witch, which industry the Millennial Generation is killing this time, and how to REALLY say it with flowers.

A fun read that will have you laughing, crying and groaning by turns, The Writing Prompt Collection is the latest in a series of Anthologies by Natasja Rose.

**Available in Kindle Ebook and Paperback**

# Cinderella Grows A Spine

Cinderella didn't know exactly what prompted her to break free of the cycle of abuse from her step-mother, but one thing was certain: nothing is ever accomplished by waiting for someone else to magically fix things.

After all, Cinderella was a pretty, educated young lady of high birth and good breeding, and her Step-mother didn't control the world, no matter what the woman thought.

It wasn't like she didn't have options...

In a delightful reinvention of the classic fairytale, Cinderella takes charge of her own destiny, and through the power of friendship, courage and liberal applications of common sense, finds her own Happily Ever After

**Book One of Timeless Tales, Modern Morals**

**Available in Kindle ebook and Paperback**

# Snow White Learns Stranger Danger

People in Fairytales are far too trusting. But what if they weren't?

Snow White learned at a young age that not everyone has good intentions, and that being a Princess didn't mean that everyone loved her.

There were people who were kind without expecting anything in return, and there probably were old beggar-women who were happy to repay a good deed, but this one was far too insistent about being allowed into the house.

In a unique re-imagining of the Classic Fairytale, Snow White learns the value of friendship, sensible precautions, and a good cast-iron skillet.
Sequel to '*Cinderella Grows a Spine*'.

**Book Two of Timeless Tales, Modern Morals**

**Available in Kindle ebook and Paperback**

# Red Riding Hood and the Stalker

Appearances can be deceiving, but a person's true nature is impossible to fully hide.

Ruby was getting very, very sick of having to hide out at her grandmothers because it was the only place Adrian Wolfe wouldn't follow her. Really, hadn't anyone ever told him that Stalking was not romantic, and that no means no?

A retelling of 'Little Red Riding Hood', in which Stalking because you "can't stay away" is a giant red flag, and the Big Bad Wolf isn't quite so obviously a Villain. Sequel to 'Snow White Learns Stranger Danger'.

**Book Three of Timeless Tales, Modern Morals**
**Available in Kindle ebook and Paperback**

# *Beautiful, Inside and Out*

What do you do when your arrogance and pride leaves you alone in the world? Some people lash out, falling deeper and deeper into darkness. Others learn from the experience, and become better for it. Isabella had never realised how much she would regret driving Sophia away, but she knew that before she could change things between them, she would need to change herself.

In a journey of self-discovery, friendship and the occasional scandal, Isabella realises that true beauty is found within, and that loving someone else is no help if you can't love yourself as well.

A 'twisted fairytale' retelling of Beauty and the Beast. Side-story to "Cinderella Grows a Spine" and "Snow White Learns Stranger Danger".

**Book Four of Timeless Tales, Modern Morals**
**Available in Kindle ebook and Paperback**

# BETWEEN DARKNESS AND LIGHT

It wasn't Jason's fault that his father's Ultimate Sacrifice hadn't resulted in Martyrdom, but in a Villainous reputation.

It wasn't Evanna's fault that she had been in the wrong place at the wrong time, and would up with Superpowers a la toxic waste.

It wasn't Stretch's fault that his teachers focused more on using his powers than on the ethics of doing so.


In a world where Superpowers are common, and those gifted with them a facet of everyday life, the lines between Hero and Villain are not always so easily drawn.

As though being a teenager wasn't hard enough!


**Book One of "Two Sides of the Same Coin"**
**Available in Paperback and Kindle ebook**

# TO LIGHT THE WAY IN DARKNESS

The first year at the Superhero Academy ended with a lot of changes, but that doesn't mean that the Super-student's problems are over.

Discrimination is still rife in the ranks, and just because things are changing doesn't mean that the underlying problems have gone away. On top of that, there are several of the 'Old Crowd' who are angry at the reluctant Superheroes as the source of all these changes, and want nothing more than to paint them as Villains.

The younger generation will need to step up their game, and keep a constant watch, if they want to survive to graduate.

**Book Two of "Two Sides of the Same Coin"**
**Available in Paperback and Kindle ebook**

# A CANDLE IN THE NIGHT

A collection of short stories based around the world and characters from the "***Two Sides of the Same Coin***" trilogy.

Read about Alien Invasions begun and ended in ways that will give future historians some very interesting days at the office, how Supervillains formed their on Council, and how DIY costumes aren't always the best idea.

From Villainous backstories, to relationships, these stories will entertain you in the best of ways.

**Side Stories from the "Two Sides of the Same Coin" Trilogy**

**Available in Paperback and Kindle ebook**

# The Time Traveller's Seamstress

Time Travel is easy. Fitting in while surfing the time-space continuum is harder.

A big part of the Time Agency's success was due to their costuming department, a variety of men and women who made fantastic clothing... and who really wished that the Agents would pay more attention to details like what year and geographical region they were heading to, and the policy on advanced notice for anything pre-1920s. Honestly, do they think all of that hand-stitched embroider and beading is easy?

A humorous read likely to make you a lot more sympathetic to the costuming department, "The Time-Traveller's Seamstress" is an entertaining book that will keep readers engaged to the end.

**Book One of Supporting the Time-Space Continuum**

**Available in Paperback and Kindle ebook**

# The Time Traveller's Seamstress

The Costuming Department probably had it worse, but life wasn't all roses in Finance, either.

Whether it was sourcing ancient coins in a usable condition, only for the Agents to lose then less than a week later, or trying to convince Management to approve a payroll system from the current century (seriously, did anyone still use paycheques for wages?), it was one problem after another.

You'd think that the other departments would be more sympathetic, given what the agents subjected them to, but no...Hilarious and relatable, this entertaining sequel to "The Time-Traveller's Seamstress" is an entertaining book that will keep readers engaged to the end.

**Book Two of Supporting the Time-Space Continuum**

**Available in Paperback and Kindle ebook**

# The Murder Mystery

Ramona Bates thought that a dating site that matched people based on their internet search history was the perfect way to get everyone off her back about her lack of a love-life. Ramona was a crime fiction writer, who was going to have a google history to match that?

When she met Joshua Ryan, a butcher's assistant who knew a surprising amount about murder, it seemed like destiny.

When Ramona released her first book, the local police force realised that a lot of the murder scenes matched with old crime reports. Now they are on the hunt, but will they catch the right person?

In a twisting tale that puts a new spin on both crime and romance, this book will have you holding your breath to the end.

**Available in Kindle Ebook and Paperback**

# Surviving a Zombie Apocalypse

No-one ever thought that the Zombie Apocalyse would actually happen.

If the average person thought about a potential Zombie Invasion at all, it was to mock unrealistic movies or discuss how/if they would survive it. That turned out to be a good thing.

When the emergency call went out that the pandemic that turned its victims into something very like Zombies was not, in fact, a viral hoax, but the real thing, they had a plan.

As it turned out, the biggest danger wasn't the Zombies, but surviving the morons who though they were living a video game and had just figured out that Loot Drops didn't exist in real life…

**Available in Kindle Ebook and Paperback**

# The Protector

All children know about the monsters. The ones under the bed, in the closet, hiding beneath the stairs... All just waiting to jump out and attack.

Children do not know of their protectors, the ones who fight the monsters, who keep the children safe, until they are no longer needed. Sometimes, that lasts a lot longer than physical childhood.

In a tale that combines that fantasy and nostalgia of childhood with the more mature outlook of adult life, The Protector is a book that will leave you longing for more.

**Available now in Kindle Ebook and Paperback**